PART II

T0083918

EASY SONGS FOR THE BEGINNING MEZZO-SOPRANO/ALTO PART II

LABORUM DULCE LENIMEN

G. SCHIRMER

Compiled by Joan Frey Boytim

Laura Ward, pianist

ISBN 978-1-4234-1214-4

G. SCHIRMER, Inc.

DISTRIBUTED BY

HAL•LEONARD®
CORPORATION

7777 W. BLUEMOUND RD. P.O. BOX 13819 MILWAUKEE, WI 53213

www.schirmer.com
www.halleonard.com

To access companion recorded accompaniments online, visit:
www.halleonard.com/mylibrary

Enter Code
6507-8774-5029-0218

PREFACE

The success of the books in the series *Easy Songs for Beginning Singers* indicates that there is a need for more preparatory literature of this type for middle school and high school singers in early stages of traditional vocal study. Teachers have commented to me that in some colleges these books are even used with very inexperienced freshmen, or with beginning adult singers.

The volumes of *Easy Songs for Beginning Singers—Part II* are at the same level as the original books. They can be used alone or in conjunction with the first set. Based on a teacher's choice of songs, there is no reason that a student could not easily start in *Part II*. Both volumes of *Easy Songs for Beginning Singers* lead very nicely into *The First Book of Solos* series (original set, *Part II*, or *Part III*).

There are 18-20 songs per volume in *Easy Songs—Part II*. A number of the selections have been out of print and will be unfamiliar to some teachers. All the songs chosen are very melodic and should pose no major musical or vocal problems for beginners of all types.

The compilation theory behind these volumes remains basically the same as in the original set. All songs are in English, some in translation, to keep the music easier to learn and comprehend. We have used songs with moderate ranges and tessituras to facilitate the building of technique. The wide variety of music includes folksongs, early show songs, operetta, parlor songs from c. 1900, as well as very easy art songs.

The art song composers include Schubert, Schumann, Franz, Arensky, Rimsky-Korsakov, Grieg, Quilter, Ireland, Head, Hopkinson, Beach and Dougherty. Operetta and vintage popular composers include Kalman, Romberg, Herbert, Berlin and Meyer. Care has been taken to provide the male voices with masculine texts. Some "old chestnuts" which young people may have never experienced include "Glow Worm," "Trees," "The Bells of St. Mary's," "Somewhere a Voice is Calling," and "Because."

My wish is that this set of books provides more options for the novice singer of any age, and helps all of my fellow teachers with the ongoing aim to lead more students into the joys of classical singing. Incidentally, these volumes may also be another source of relaxed and fun material for experienced singers.

Joan Frey Boytim
May, 2006

CONTENTS

The price of this publication includes access to companion recorded piano accompaniments online, for download or streaming, using the unique code found on the title page.
Visit **www.halleonard.com/mylibrary** and enter the access code.

THE BONNY LIGHTER-BOY

English Folksong

Collected and arranged by
Cecil J. Sharp
(1859-1924)

Allegretto grazioso

1. It's _ of a brisk _ young sail - or lad, And he ap - pren - tice bound; ___ And she a mer-chant's daugh - ter, With fif - ty thou - sand pound ___ They loved each oth - er dear - ly, In sor - row and in joy: ___ Let him go where he will, he's my love still, He's my bon - ny light - er - boy. ___

in my fa - ther's gar - den, Be - neath the wil - low tree, ___ He took me up all in his arms, And kissed me ten - der - ly ___ Down on the ground we both sat down, And talked of love and joy: ___ Let him say what he will, he's my love still, He's my bon - ny light - er - boy. ___

1.

2. 'Twas _

3. Her _ fa - ther, he be-ing near her, He heard what she did say _____ He

cried: Un - ru - ly daugh - ter, I'll send him far _ a - way; _____ On

board a ship I'll have him pressed, I'll rob you of your joy: _____ Send him

where you will, he's my love still, He's my bon - ny light - er - boy. _____

CRADLE SONG

Anton Arensky
(1861-1906)

Sleep, my dar - ling, have no fear, for thy Moth - er watch - es near. By her side as day is done, the ea - gle, wind ____ and the sun.

To his nest the ea - gle flies.

O'er the hill the sun - light dies. All the night the faith - ful breeze

mur - mured low a - mong the trees. _____

"Lit - tle breeze, now tell me, pray, Why were you so ___ long a - way?

Did you put the stars to sleep, Rock the bil - lows on the deep?"

"By a cra - dle all night long

I have crooned my slum - ber song.

For a lit - tle child; and he Now lies sleep - ing _ qui - et - ly."

JOHNNY HAS GONE FOR A SOLDIER

American Revolutionary War Song
Based on a 17th Century Irish tune
Arranged by Richard Walters

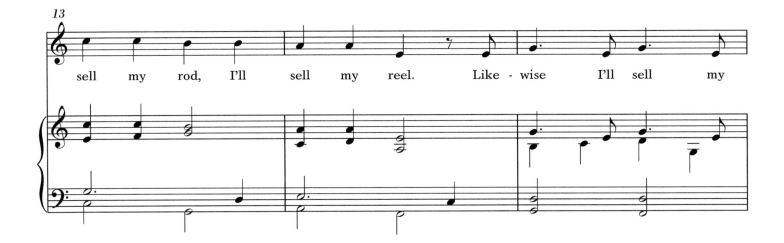

sell my rod, I'll sell my reel. Like - wise I'll sell my

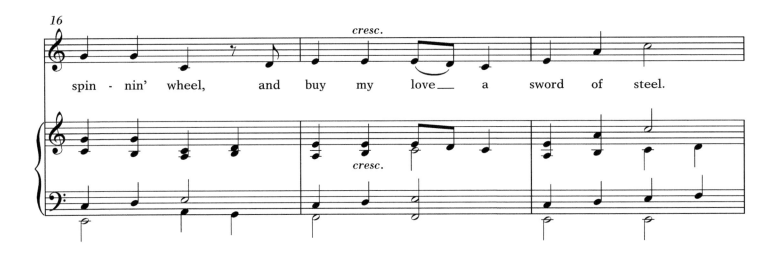

spin - nin' wheel, and buy my love___ a sword of steel.

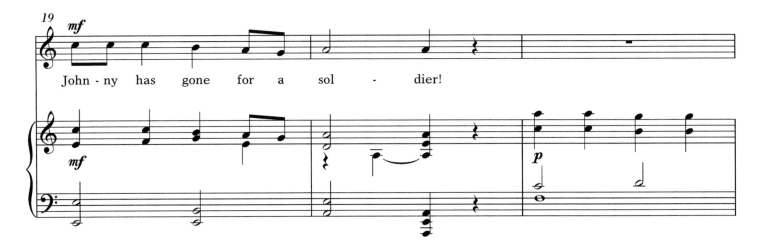

John - ny has gone for a sol - dier!

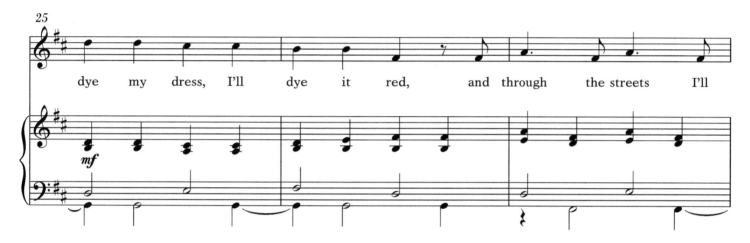

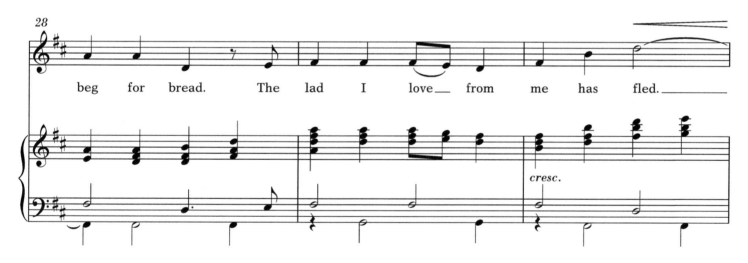

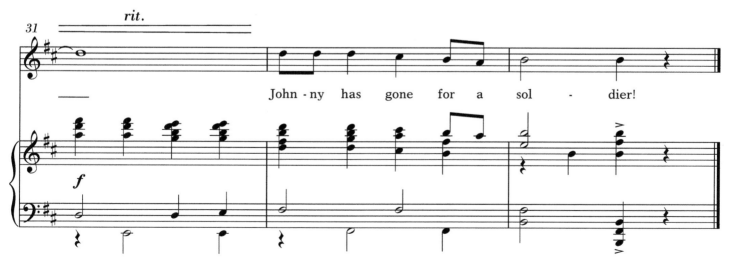

GO FROM MY WINDOW, GO

16th Century Air,
adapted by Harold Boulton

Arranged by
Arthur Somervell
(1863-1937)

go, You took a lov - er new, And she wears a rose what -

ev - er way she _ goes, While I noth-ing wear but rue. Go from my win - dow,

go, Go for a day and a year, And then if you woo, And I

deem your heart is _ true, You at last shall be lodg - ed here.

KISS ME AGAIN

Henry Blossom

Victor Herbert
(1859-1924)

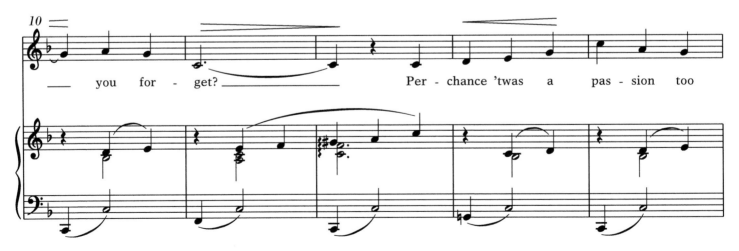

won - drous to last, But I dream _____ of it yet! _____

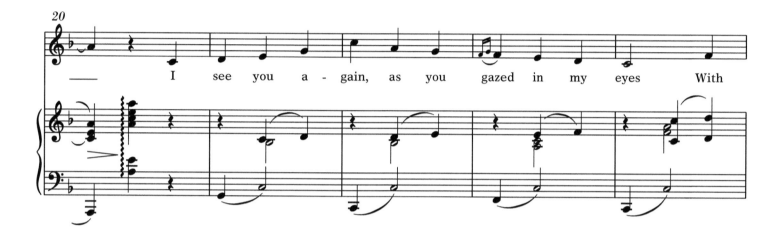

_____ I see you a - gain, as you gazed in my eyes With

joy _____ all a - light! _____ So fond - ly you'd

rit.

fold me as soft - ly you told me Of Love through the star - sprin - kled

Valse lente

night. _____ Sweet sum - mer breeze, whis - per - ing

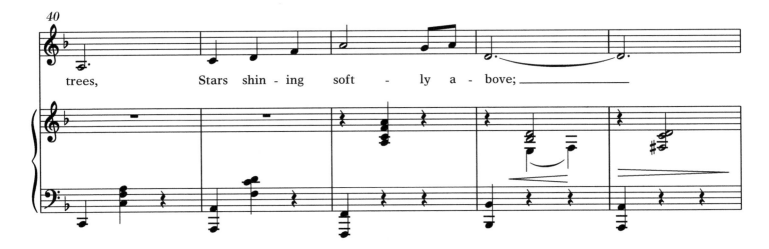

trees, Stars shin - ing soft - ly a - bove; _____

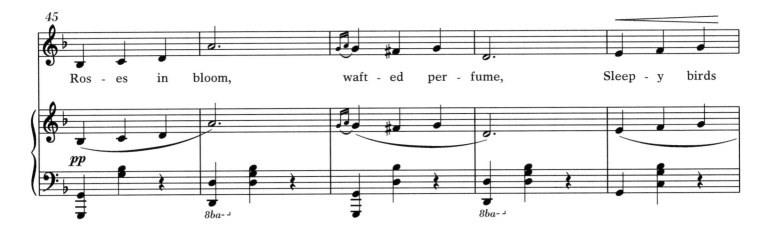

Ros - es in bloom, waft - ed per - fume, Sleep - y birds

dream - ing of love. _____ Safe in your arms,

far from a - larms, Day-light shall come but in vain.

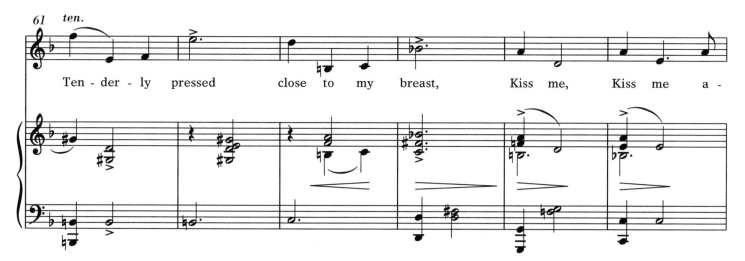

Ten - der - ly pressed close to my breast, Kiss me, Kiss me a -

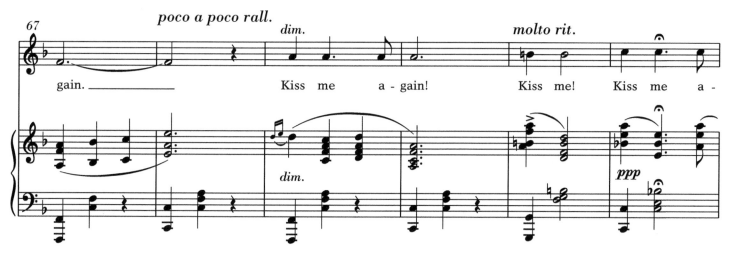

gain. Kiss me a - gain! Kiss me! Kiss me a -

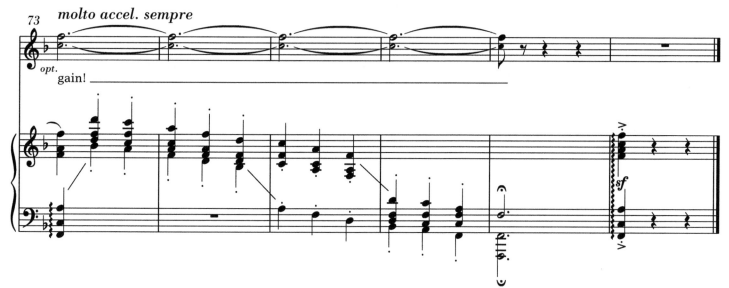

gain!

LITTLE BOY BLUE

Eugene Field

Ethelbert Nevin
(1862-1901)

dog was new, And the sol - dier was pass - ing fair;_____ And that was the time when our

dolce

lit - tle Boy Blue _____ Kissed them, and put them there._____ "Now don't you go till I

distinto ma p

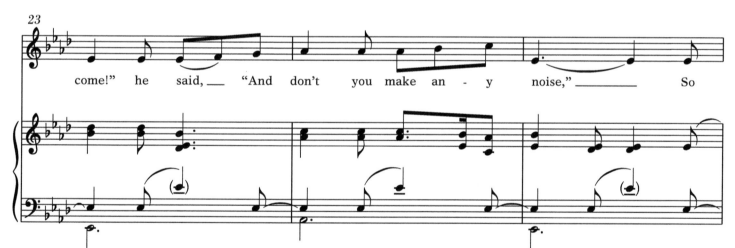

come!" he said, ___ "And don't you make an - y noise," _____ So

todd - ling off to his trun - dle bed, ___ He dreamt of the pret - ty

toys. _____ And as he was dream-ing, an an - gel song A -

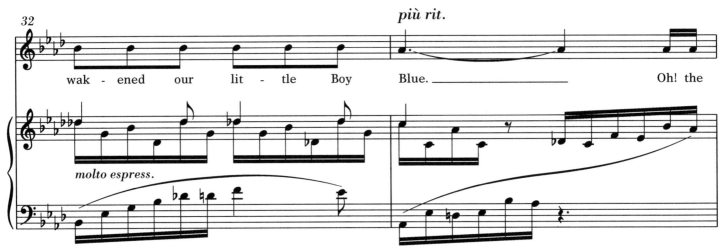

wak - ened our lit - tle Boy Blue. _____ Oh! the

years _ are man - y, the years _ are long, But our lit - tle toy friends are

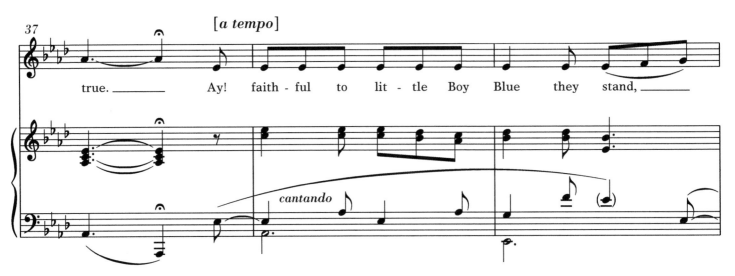

true. _____ Ay! faith - ful to lit - tle Boy Blue they stand, _____

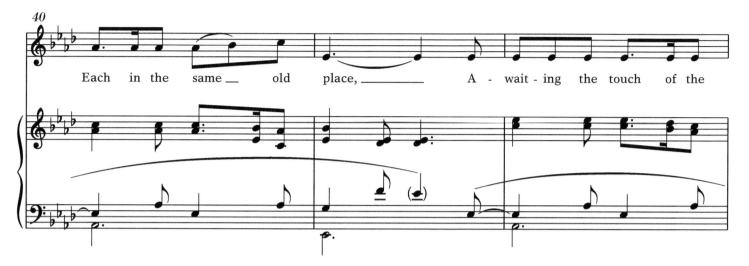

Each in the same__ old place,_____ A - wait-ing the touch of the

lit - tle hand,__ The smile of a lit - tle face._____ And they

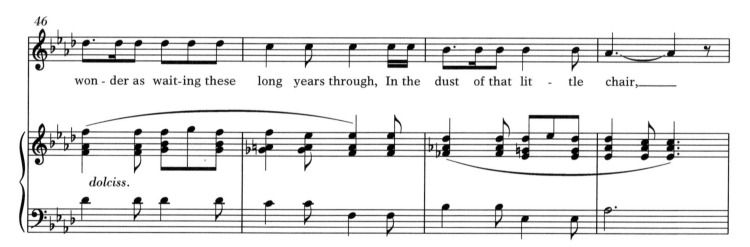

won - der as wait-ing these long years through, In the dust of that lit - tle chair,__

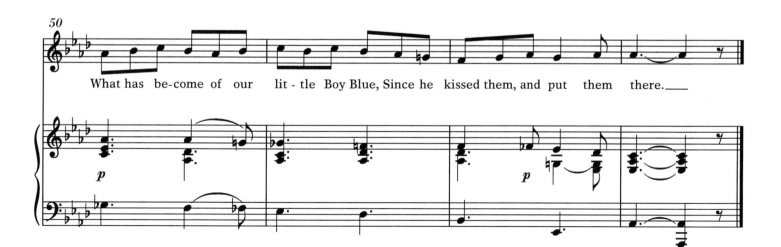

What has be-come of our lit - tle Boy Blue, Since he kissed them, and put them there.__

LOVE'S OWN SWEET SONG

C.C.S. Cushing and
E.P. Heath

Emmerich Kálmán
(1882-1953)

Tempo di Valse

In the toils of love I'm caught, _____ Hap - pi -
Love to us has lent his wings, _____ To the

you,   No   one else will do,   Love   and love a - lone   is all to

glide,   Ev - er at your side,   You   shall be my bride   what er'e be -

blame. _____

tide. _____ } Oh let   us   come   and   dance with

joy   Since love   and life   are   ours, _____   For

youth   is strong   and blood   grows warm   Be - neath   the

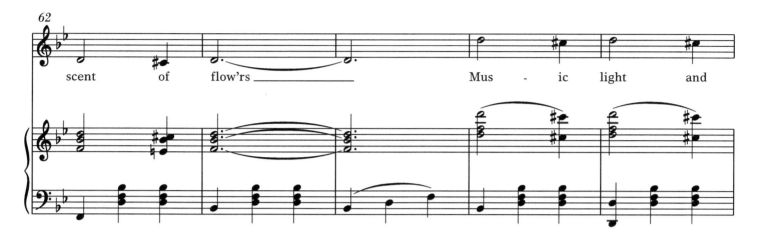

scent of flow'rs _____ Mus - ic light and

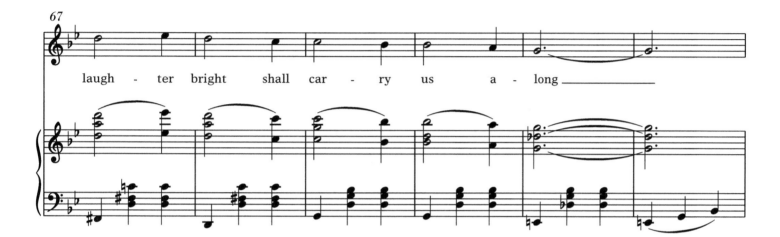

laugh - ter bright shall car - ry us a - long _____

poco animato

Sing - ing with our hearts on fire love's own

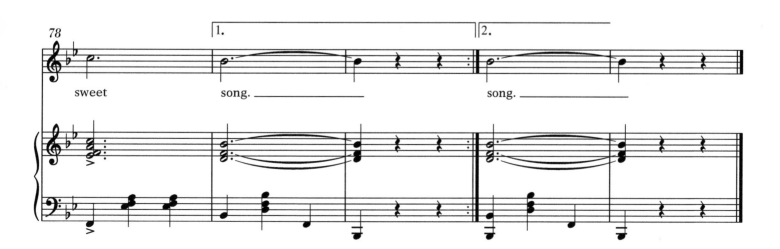

sweet song. _____ song. _____

JUST FOR THIS

Cora Fabbri

Amy Marcy Cheney Beach
(1867-1944)

Allegretto à capriccio

Just a mul - ti - tude _ of _ curls

Weigh - ing down a lit - tle _ head; _ Two wide eyes not

blue _ nor _ gray, Like the _ sky 'twixt night _ and _ day,

Small red mouth and

all — to — say Has been said.

Just a sauc - y

word — or — glance, And a hand held out — to — kiss; —

Just a curl a rib - bon _ through   Just a ___ flow - er

fresh _ and _ blue...

And to think what men will do ___ Just for this!

THE MISSION OF A ROSE

G. Clifton Bingham

Frederic H. Cowen
(1852-1935)

out in the world. There in her sim - ple dress it lay,

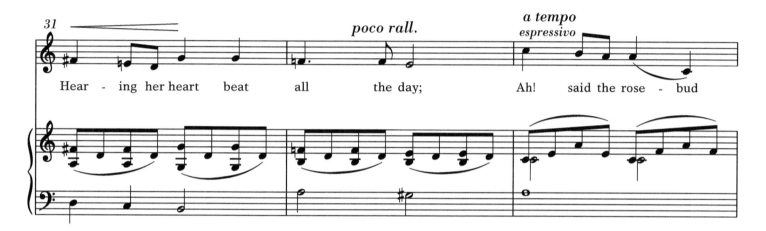

Hear - ing her heart beat all the day; Ah! said the rose - bud

now let me break In - to a rose for her __ sweet sake.

But still a bud it was giv'n a - way, a sick child saw it from

where she lay, It brought to the pale sad face a smile, _____

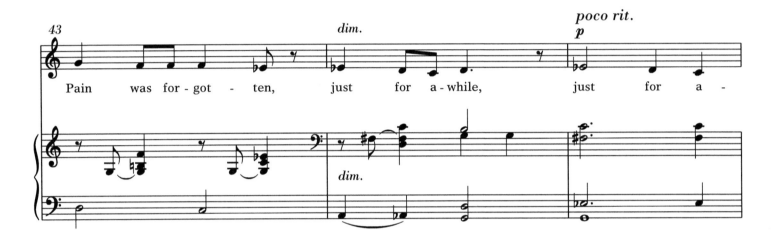

Pain was for-got-ten, just for a-while, just for a-

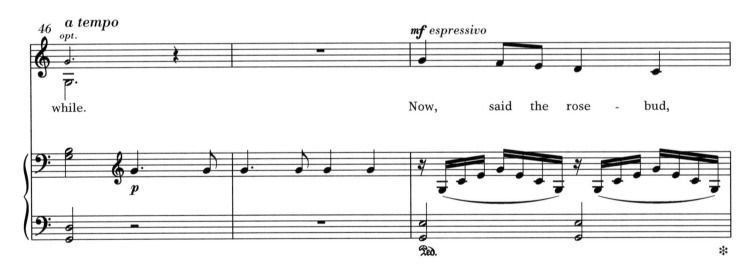

while. Now, said the rose-bud,

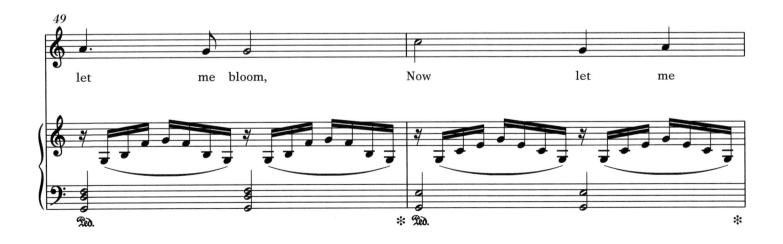

let me bloom, Now let me

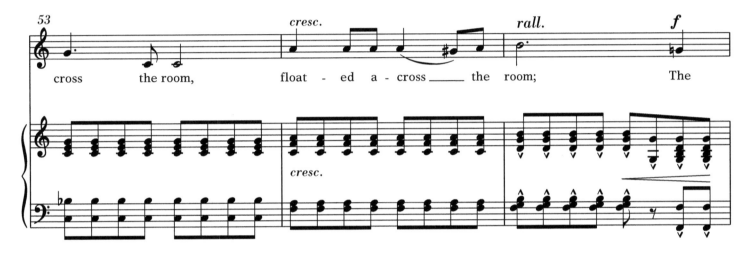

MY DAYS HAVE BEEN SO WONDROUS FREE

Thomas Parnell

Francis Hopkinson
(1737-1791)

Allegretto grazioso ♩ = 88

poco rit.

a tempo
mp

days have ___ been so ___ won - drous free, The ___

lit - tle ___ birds ___ that fly With ___ care - less

ease from __ tree __ to tree, Were __ but as __ blest as __

poco rit.   *a tempo*

I, Were __ but __ as blest as I!

colla voce

poco più mosso

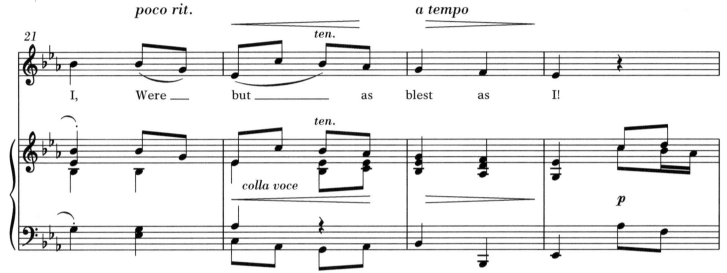

Ask __ glid - ing wat - ers

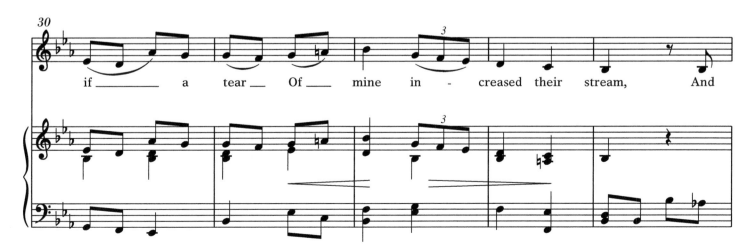

if __ a tear __ Of __ mine in - creased their stream, And

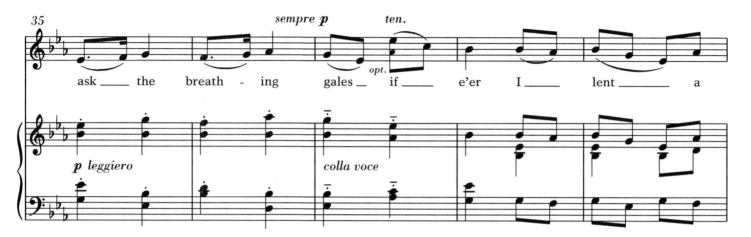

ask ___ the breath - ing gales ___ if ___ e'er I ___ lent ___ a

sigh to them, _____ I ___ lent ___ a ___ sigh to

them!

PHILOSOPHY

David Emmell

Allegretto grazioso

A bee once 'light-ed on a flow'r,

All on a sum-mer day, _____ He sipped it once, he sipped it

twice, And then he flew a-way. There

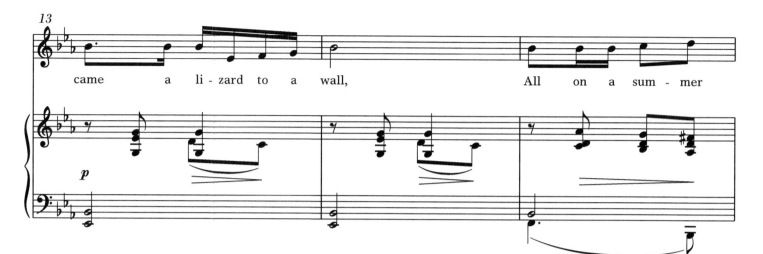

came a li-zard to a wall, All on a sum - mer

day, _____ He ven-tured once, he ven-tured twice, And

then he ran a - way. There came a lov - er to a

maid, All on a sum - mer day, _____ He kissed her

once, he kissed her twice, And then he rode a - way._____

_____ For the flow'r had no ho - ney, The wall was - n't

rall.   *a tempo*

sun - ny, And the maid had no mon - ey, Is - n't it

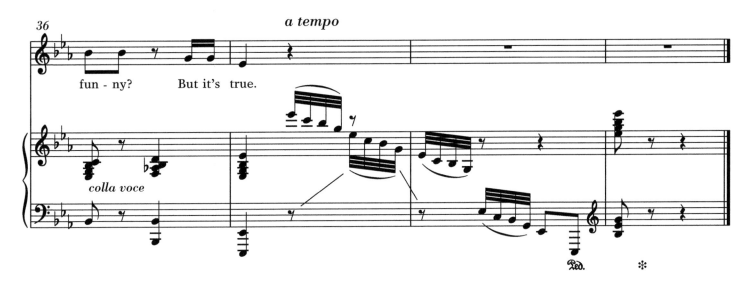

a tempo

fun - ny? But it's true.

SECOND HAND ROSE

Grant Clarke

James F. Hanley
(1892-1942)

a - no in the par - lor
ja - mas when I don 'em

Fa - ther bought for
have some - bod - y

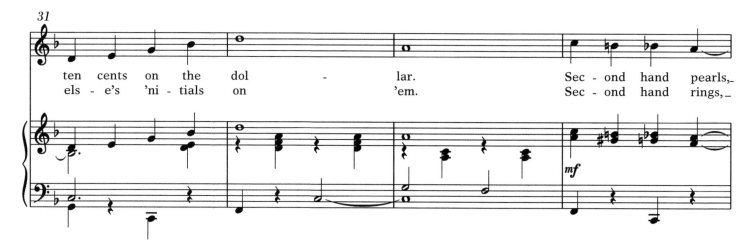

ten cents on the dol - lar.
els - e's 'ni - tials on 'em.

Sec - ond hand pearls,
Sec - ond hand rings,

___ I'm wear - ing sec - ond hand curls. ___
___ I'm sick of sec - ond hand things. ___

I nev - er get a
I nev - er get what

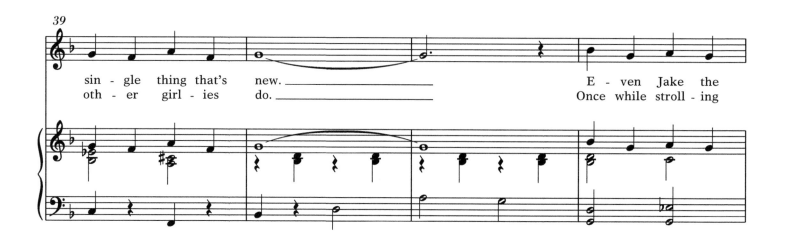

sin - gle thing that's new. ___
oth - er girl - ies do. ___

E - ven Jake the
Once while stroll - ing

SOFT-FOOTED SNOW

Helge Rode
English version by Robert A. Sickert

Sigurd Lie
(1871-1904)

There is nought on earth as pure ___ as the ___ snow! ___

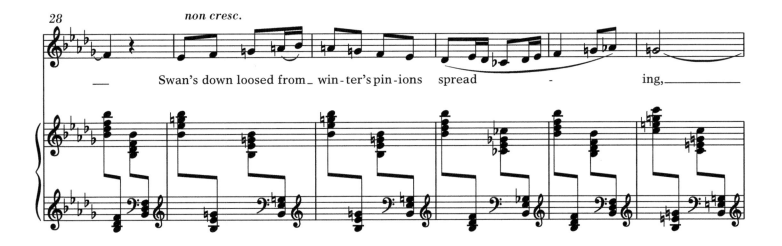

non cresc.

___ Swan's down loosed from ___ win-ter's pin-ions spread ___ ing, ___

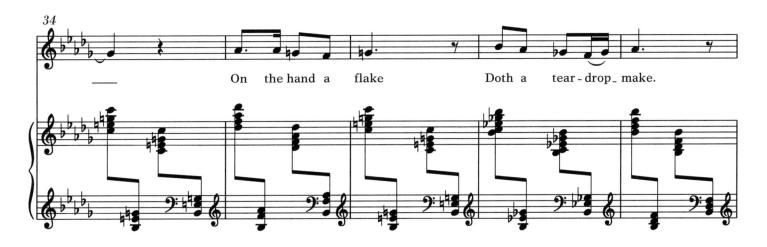

On the hand a flake Doth a tear-drop ___ make.

non cresc.

Through the crys-tal ___ air white thoughts are thread ___ ing. ___

Nought so lull-ing on the earth — as the — snow! _____

non cresc.

Sink-ing light as — slum-ber on the wea - ry _____

Till the si-lence so in - to sound doth — grow, Fine as sil - ver — bells, a mu-sic

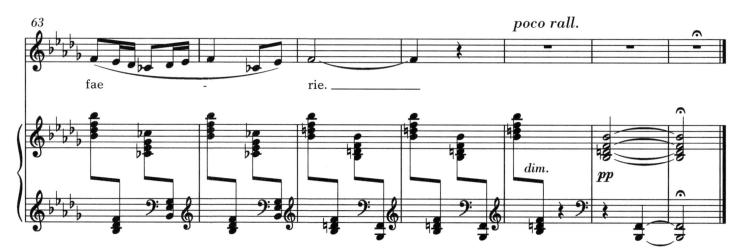

poco rall.

fae - rie. _____

dim.

pp

SOLDIER, SOLDIER WILL YOU MARRY ME?

American Folksong
Arranged by Brian Dean

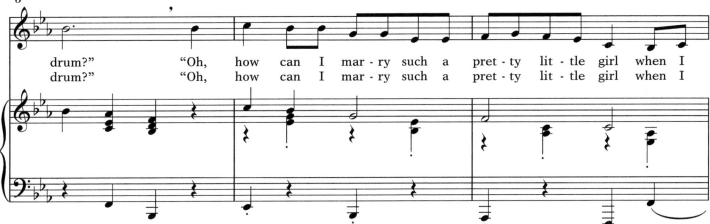

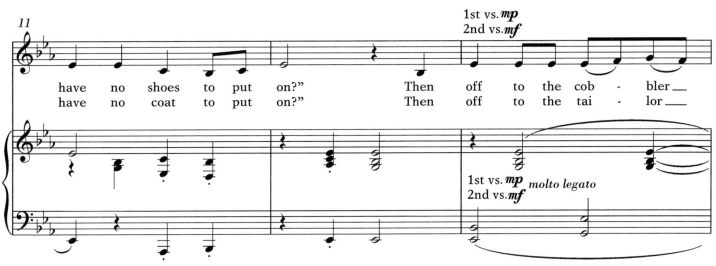

fast as she___ could___ run. She brought him back the

fin - est that was there and the sol - dier put it___ on.

4. "Now

sol - dier, sol - dier will you mar - ry me with your mus - ket, fife and

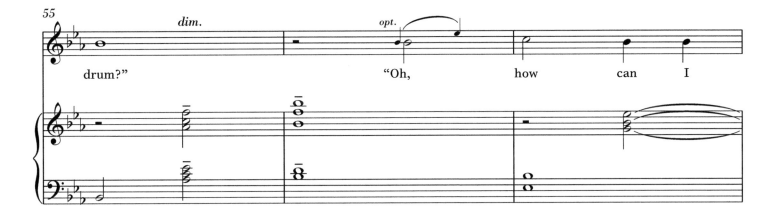

drum?" "Oh, how can I

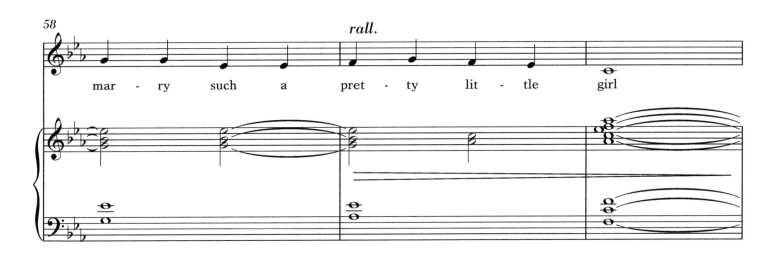

mar - ry such a pret - ty lit - tle girl

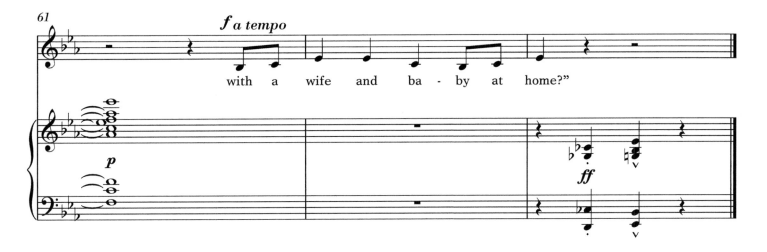

with a wife and ba - by at home?"

SPRING SORROW

Rupert Brooke

John Ireland
(1879-1962)

Poco andante

All sud - den - ly the wind comes soft, And

Spring is here a - gain; And the haw-thorn quick - ens with buds of green, And my

heart with buds of pain. My heart all Win - ter lay so numb, The

earth so dead and frore, That I nev-er thought the Spring would come, Or my

heart wake a-ny more. But Win-ter's bro-ken and earth has

wok-en, And the small birds cry a-gain; And the haw-thorn hedge puts

forth its buds And my heart puts forth its pain.

THE STRANGER-MAN

Arthur Macy

George Whitefield Chadwick
(1854-1931)

Now what is this,_ my_ daugh - ter dear, Up - on thy cheek so

fair? 'Tis but a kiss, my moth-er dear, Kind for - tune sent it

there; It was a cour - teous strang - er-man That gave_ it un - to

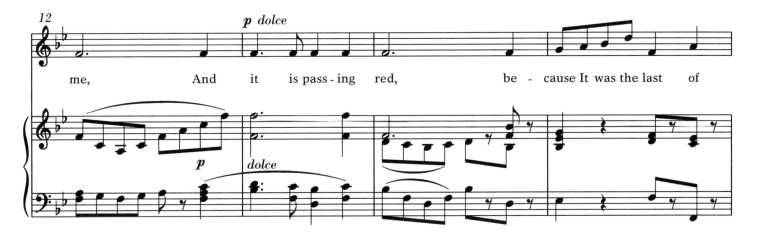

me, And it is pass - ing red, be - cause It was the last of

three. A kiss, in-deed, my

daugh - ter dear! I___ mar - vel in sur - prise! Such

con - duct with a strang - er-man, I fear me, was not wise. Me -

27 *a tempo*

thought the same, my moth - er — dear, And so at three for - bore, Al -

31 *animato*

though the cour - teous strang - er - man Vowed he — had — man - y more.

35 *p*

Now

38

prith - ee, daugh - ter, — quick - ly go And — bring the strang - er

here, And bid him hie and bid him fly To

me,___ my daugh-ter dear; For times be ver - y,

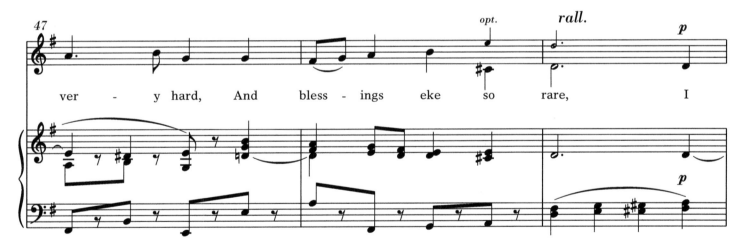

ver - y hard, And bless - ings eke so rare, I

fain would meet a strang-er-man That hath a kiss to spare.

A SWAN

Henrik Ibsen
English version by Frederic Field Bullard

Edvard Grieg
(1843-1907)

My swan, my treas - ure, With snow-y-white feath - er,

Of his songs sang me nev - er A sin - gle meas - ure.

Shy - ly, fear - ing the elves in the brush - es,

'TWAS IN THE LOVELY MONTH OF MAY
(Im wunderschönen Monat Mai)

Heinrich Heine
English version by Arthur Westbrook

Robert Schumann
(1810-1856)

con Pedale

'Twas in the love-ly month of May, When all the buds___ were blow - ing, I felt with-in my bos - om The flame of love was glow - ing.

'Twas in the love-ly month of May, When all the birds ___ were sing - ing, I came un - to my dar - ling, My love and long - ing bring - ing.

SOMEWHERE A VOICE IS CALLING

Eileen Newton

Arthur F. Tate
(1870-1950)

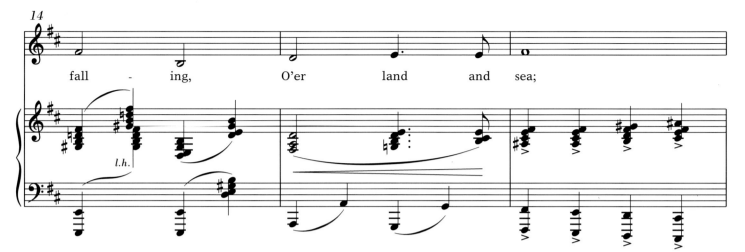

14

fall - ing, O'er land and sea;

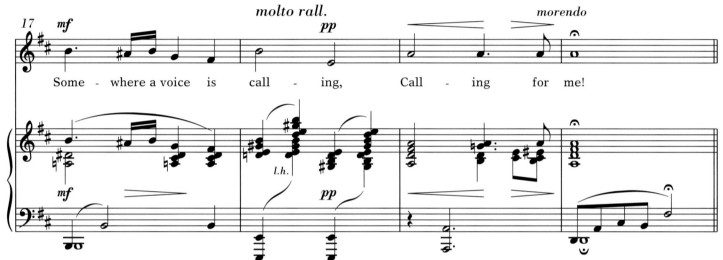

17 mf

molto rall. pp *morendo*

Some - where a voice is call - ing, Call - ing for me!

21 *a tempo* *rit.*

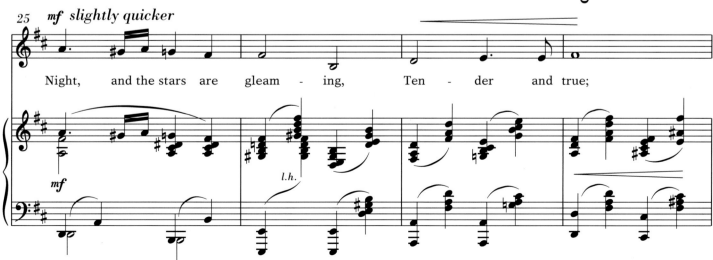

25 mf *slightly quicker*

Night, and the stars are gleam - ing, Ten - der and true;